In Everglade Studio

Nathaniel Brimmer-Beller

methuen | drama

LONDON • NEW YORK • OXFORD • NEW DELHI • SYDNEY

METHUEN DRAMA
Bloomsbury Publishing Plc
50 Bedford Square, London, WC1B 3DP, UK
1385 Broadway, New York, NY 10018, USA
29 Earlsfort Terrace, Dublin 2, Ireland

BLOOMSBURY, METHUEN DRAMA and the Methuen
Drama logo are trademarks of Bloomsbury Publishing Plc

First published in Great Britain 2024

Cover design by Holly Capper

Cover image © rob dobi/Getty Images

A catalogue record for this book is available from the British Library.

A catalog record for this book is available from the Library of Congress.

ISBN: PB: 978-1-3504-9676-7
ePDF: 978-1-3504-9677-4
eBook: 978-1-3504-9678-1

Series: Modern Plays

Typeset by Mark Heslington Ltd, Scarborough, North Yorkshire

To find out more about our authors and books visit
www.bloomsbury.com and sign up for our newsletters.

In Everglade Studio was performed at the Hope Theatre in London in April 2024. The cast and creative team were as follows:

Writer, Lyricist, Co-Director and Clarke: Nathaniel Brimmer-Beller

Co-Director: Phoebe Rowell John

Musical Director, Composer and Baron: Aveev Isaacson

Skye: Emily Moment

Matilda: Hannah Omisore

Pictured, from left to right: Nathaniel Brimmer-Beller, Emily Moment and Hannah Omisore.

Nathaniel Brimmer-Beller | Writer, Lyricist, Clarke and Co-Director

Nathaniel Brimmer-Beller is a playwright, actor and director originally from Washington, DC, now living in the United Kingdom. He has directed more than thirty theatrical productions and has written fifteen plays, including six acclaimed premieres at the Edinburgh Fringe Festival.

His play *Blood Red Apples and Deep Gold Honey* was nominated for the George Devine Award for Most Promising Playwright in 2022. This philosophical comedy-drama explored his mixed-race and Jewish heritage and was developed through the Almeida Theatre's Anthem project.

His Edinburgh Fringe plays have transferred to London on multiple occasions – most notably his darkly comedic political satire *Chagos 1971* in 2019, and his fast-paced Hollywood awards-industry satire *Press* in 2021 and 2022, which has returned to London stages four times since. Nathaniel portrayed that play's lead character David Fring in all of these productions. In 2023, he developed David's personality into a monologue performance which earned him a Bursary Prize at the writer-performer competition Screenshot, organised by South of the River Pictures and SISTER Global. After the competition, panel judge Olivia Colman called Nathaniel 'a f**king great actor'. This he will not soon forget.

Also in 2023, he brought *In Everglade Studio* to the Edinburgh Fringe for a month-long run, where the play was longlisted for the BBC Writersroom Popcorn Award for Best New Writing.

Other recent works written by Nathaniel include 1960s-set fashion-industry mystery *Nines* and satire of the contemporary theatre industry *The Kindness of Strangers*, both of which enjoyed successful runs at the Canal Café Theatre. *The Kindness of Strangers*, originally developed as a double-bill with *Press*, transferred to VAULT Festival in 2023.

Nathaniel wrote, directed and edited the short film *Evening Plans* in 2021, which was nominated for Best Short Film in the New Visions category at the Edinburgh International Film Festival. He also wrote the radio play *Turner & Turner* and acclaimed Edinburgh Fringe plays *Mack the Knife*, *Technicolor* and *Fear of Roses*.

Nathaniel studied International Relations at the University of Edinburgh and received an MA with Distinction in Film Studies from King's College London.

Nathaniel continues to write plays, films and more, and looks forward to bringing works such as *The Net Under Makeout Bridge*, *London Fog*, *Signora Sorelli* and *The Hampstead Cage* to life in the near future.

Phoebe Rowell John | Co-Director

Phoebe is a London-based director who began making theatre as part of Chickenshed's Young Company. She went on to direct a range of productions while studying History at the University of Cambridge, including Shakespeare, a musical and other contemporary classics. She then completed an MA in Theatre Directing at Mountview. As part of her final showcase, she adapted two sixteenth-century texts into a new play *The Woman-Hater.* This project combined her main interests in using the past to explore the present and investigating gender and power through theatre. She is the current Resident Assistant Director for London Youth Theatre.

Her directing credits include: *Not Dead But Growing* (Applecart Arts); *The Intricate Art of Actually Caring* (Hope Theatre); *Press* (Old Red Lion); *The Woman-Hater* (The Backstage Theatre, Mountview); *Love and Information* (Studio, Mountview); *Guys and Dolls* (ADC Theatre); *Romeo and Juliet* (ADC Theatre); *Crouch, Touch, Pause, Engage* (Corpus Playroom) and *Escaped Alone* (Corpus Playroom).

Her assistant directing credits include: *Horizon* (LYT, Seven Dials Playhouse); *Trashomon* (Short Film); *rob steal swindle* (The Backstage Theatre, Mountview); *Mary Poppins* (Studio, Mountview); *A View from the Bridge* (ADC Theatre); *Antigone* (Corpus Playroom); *In the Next Room (or The Vibrator Play)* (ADC Theatre) and *Saint Joan* (ADC Theatre).

Aveev Isaacson | Musical Director, Composer and Baron

Aveev is an actor, composer and director of Jewish-Russian heritage. In his early years, he studied piano and composition and later specialised in History of Theatre at Thelma-Yellin School for the Arts. He then moved to the UK to train as an actor with Mountview.

Recently he made his debut as music director for *NewsRevue* Canal Café Theatre), wrote and directed the short *Worst Treated Things* (The Unseen), and composed original music for a bilingual production of Brecht's *The Chalk Circle*, set in 1930s Palestine and performed in both Arabic and Hebrew (Goodman School of Acting).

He continues to work internationally on and off-stage, recently as an assistant director on productions of *Salome*, *Carmen* and *Tosca* (The Israeli Opera).

Emily Moment | Skye

Emily Moment is a North American actress and singer/songwriter based in London. After starting in regional playhouses and youth Shakespeare companies, her professional theatrical training was undertaken at The British American Drama Academy in Oxford and Wagner College Performing Arts in New York City, where she worked in stage and film productions for thirteen years before permanently relocating to the UK. As a musician, she has released a solo full-length Americana album, *The Party's Over* (2021), as well as four albums and several singles with folk-rock band, Mahoney & The Moment.

Her musical performances have been featured on BBC One, BBC Radio 4 and Radio 6. Emily is thrilled to be making her British theatre debut with *In Everglade Studio*.

Hannah Omisore | Matilda

Hannah is a Nigerian-British actress based in London who spent time at IDSA, exploring screen, text, voice and movement, as well as partaking in an eight-month theatre program at Talawa Theatre Company. As a storyteller, she is interested in exploring complex and diverse writing and characters through acting, movement and singing on stage and screen. Credits include: *The Skin I Move In* (BBC New Creatives); *Stand Up* (London Film School) and *In Everglade Studio* (Mountview MA Directors' Showcase; Assembly, Edinburgh Fringe Festival).

About Black Bat Productions

Black Bat Productions makes theatre that's original, fast-paced, stylish, and, often, set in the past. Since its founding in 2017, Black Bat plays have frequently revisited the 1950s, 1960s and 1970s, allowing for memorable and creative soundtracks, visuals and costume designs, yet the subject matter never loses sight of issues facing contemporary society today.

In playing with the past, Black Bat aims to address the audience's present while giving them a very good time and a piece of theatre both entertaining to watch and likely to start conversations afterwards.

In addition to multiple London runs, Black Bat Productions has staged original work at the Edinburgh Fringe Festival seven times. Notable productions include the premiere runs of *Press* ('Genius . . . pleasurably wicked' – Monica Yell, *Broadway Baby*; 'Fringe theatre does not get much better than this' – Violet Mackintosh, *The Violet Curtain*), of *Chagos 1971* ('The most intelligent piece of theatre I have seen at the Fringe' – Annabel Jackson, *EdFringe Review*), and of *In Everglade Studio* ('an intelligently constructed masterpiece' – Jemima Hawkins, *The Student*).

In recommending *Fear of Roses* in 2021, AllEdinburgh Theatre wrote of Black Bat Productions: 'Anyone who has seen one of their previous productions will recognise several of the elements on display . . . a noirish sheen, taut and snappy dialogue, a clever script with well-engineered twists, an almost miraculous cool.' In recommending *In Everglade Studio* in 2023, calling it 'Nathaniel Brimmer-Beller's most impressive piece to date,' AllEdinburgh Theatre wrote: 'As was the case with previous Black Bat productions, there is both a polished surface . . . and a profound undercurrent.'

Black Bat Productions continues to make work, in London and elsewhere.

In Everglade Studio

For Doris,
and for Esther,
and for Andy,
and Steven and Hermi and Mickey.

Thank you.
I would not be where I am, and doing this, if not for all of you.

And thank you to W-BIG 100.3 FM.
What a difference a song makes.

Ride around them dogies, ride around them slow
They're fiery and snuffy and rarin' to go

Goodbye, old paint
I'm leavin' Cheyenne

– Charley Willis

Characters

Skye, *a young white woman, English*
Matilda, *a young black woman, English*
Baron, *a cynical young man, from the British Isles*
Clarke, *a mixed-race man, American*

Place: *Five floors underground in Everglade Studio, in the forgotten London area Burton Ames.*

Time: *August, 1974.*

A note on the goings-on: *Everyone in Everglade Studio completely loses their inhibitions by the play's end, slowly but surely, one way or another. Consider all the freedom, horror and potential this implies and make of that what you will.*

In Everglade Studio is indebted to many disparate inspirations, ranging from The Kinks' mid-60s televised performances to Jeremy Saulnier's *Green Room* to a sunny mid-afternoon walk in 2020. From the air in record store basements to the concept of directing theatre as a mixed-race Jew to John Prine's debut album, *John Prine*. From Aretha Franklin to Colter Wall to Charley Crockett, from John Brown to Nat Turner, from Armando Iannucci to Richard C. Sarafian's *Vanishing Point*, to a white horse named Justin and a cat named Ernie.

Thank you to everyone involved directly and indirectly, for your help in pulling all this and more together.

Love,

NBB

Act One

Low lights illuminate Everglade Studio. Two microphones on stands, a keyboard, a few stools, a few music stands and a makeshift recording booth to the side.

This is not the crème de la crème of the recording industry.

Skye *is seated centre stage on a stool. She is preparing to record. Getting in the mindset.*

Skye *is a young singer, British but styles herself like an American Southern belle. White. Trying to be Dolly Parton and not doing so badly.*

Baron *sits at the keyboard in the background, waiting. Waiting for* **Skye**'*s mindset to kick in.*

Baron *is a session player, used to working with just about everyone and connecting with just about no one. Can play every instrument in that room and has at one point or another. But he's tired of this nomadic routine.*

Clarke *fixes up details around the studio.*

Clarke *is* **Skye**'*s manager; she is his latest long-shot attempt at turning obscure talent into stardom and by far the most successful – due more to her ruthlessness than his management. But they make a good, if flawed, team.*

Skye *runs this room, because* **Skye**'*s career runs* **Clarke**.

When **Skye** *is ready,* **Clarke** *sits behind the recording desk. Lights dim.*

One

'Terror Underground: Return To Everglade Studio'

The audio track from a documentary is heard, reverberating in the room. Its aural quality is lacking, regular spots and skips plague the recording. It hasn't been played in decades.

As it plays, the lights slowly come up in the studio.

Skye *is situated, at the ready.* **Clarke** *waves to* **Baron** *and gestures at* **Skye***.* **Baron** *shrugs, gestures at her himself.* **Clarke** *looks at* **Skye***.* **Skye** *repositions and gets ready to sing.* **Clarke** *gets the desk ready.*

Over this, we hear the documentary's audio.

Documentary (*voiceover*)
We know so much about the wonders
and creative heights reached in the
recording studios of London during
this period, but so little is known
about their darkest moments.
Including occurrences in the late
hours of one August evening in
1974. We know the studio, we know
it closed, we know it closed
suddenly, and we know all the tapes
recorded its final night of use
were ordered to be destroyed by a
High Court judge so they cannot
fall into public consumption. And
yet, the story of what happened in
Everglade Studio has not yet been
fully explored. We intend to do
that now. So join us as –

The crackly audio cuts out.

Clarke *gives* **Baron** *a thumbs-up and hits record.*

A red lightbulb on the wall illuminates.

Two

8:03pm

The first chord of 'When Things Went South' – **Skye** *sings and plays guitar,* **Baron** *plays piano.*

Skye (*singing*)
    Call 'em, call 'em neighbor
    The colts are running wild
    Call 'em call 'em neighbor
    Got a day of tanning hide
    I ain't got no time
    I've left the world behind
    When things went south
    My lover'd gone
    The road to hell looked fine
    Call 'em call 'em reverend
    The ghosts of this new land
    Have raised a friendly wager
    I can't hack it like a man
    Call 'em call 'em reverend
    Don't you dare to let 'em think
    This ropin' hopin' lady's
    Better off at home in pink
    In other words I ain't got no time
    I've left the world behind
    When things went south
    My lover'd gone
    The road to hell looked fine
    Tell 'em tell 'em cowboys
    Tell 'em call me Skye
    Better yet call me Missus
    Best yet make yourself my wives
    Got a trail of drooling cowpokes
    Followin' long on bended knee
    They'd kiss my boots
    They'd treat me right
    If I ever had the time
    But don't they know
    I ain't got no time
    I've left the world behind
    When things went south
    My lover'd gone
    The road to hell looked fine

Baron *plays the instrumental break.*

Skye (*singing*)
   The sky's the limit
   My heart's done set
   On this way of living life
   Ain't no cowboy's candied arm
   Ain't no homely wife
   I ain't no got time
   I've left the world behind
   When things went south
   My lover'd gone
   And the road to hell looked fine
   When things went south
   My lover'd gone
   When things went south
   My lover, my lover'd gone
   When things went south
   My lover'd gone
   My lover'd gone
   When things went south!
   When things went south
   My lover'd gone
   The road to hell looked fine!

Matilda *walks into the studio in the last few seconds of the performance.*

Matilda *is a young Black woman, dressed like it's just a few years earlier, still emulating the 60s girl groups. Slightly awed by the studio, but quickly mortified that she has interrupted.*

Matilda
   Oh! My apologies!

The song unceremoniously clatters to a halt.

Clarke, *who has been sketching out a plan for the evening the whole time, doesn't notice, then, hearing the music is finished, stops the recording.*

The red bulb goes out.

Baron
You cannot be serious.

Matilda
I can go back out?

Skye (*not looking at* **Matilda**)
We're recording, honey.

Matilda
Oh god.

Baron
But by all means, go back out.

Matilda
This is –

Skye
Everglade. You found it. As far
down as you can go.

Baron
In so many ways.

Skye
In the building, Baron.

Baron
Right.

Skye
He meant the building.

Clarke *steps out from behind his desk. He fawns over* **Skye**.

Clarke
Brilliant, brilliant, what can I
say.

Skye
Even with?

Clarke
Even with what?

Skye *and* **Baron** *gesture at* **Matilda**. **Clarke** *notices her and beams.*

Clarke
Is this THE Matilda?!

Matilda
Matilda Stokes, hello.

Clarke
Hello, sister! Welcome to your
musical future. Come here!

Clarke *gestures for* **Matilda** *to come further into the room.*

Matilda
Oh – hi.

She advances slightly. **Clarke** *gazes at her – welcoming and hungry.*

Clarke
Skye, Baron, this woman and her
mind for music might just take us
to the top.

Skye
Wow.

Baron
How?

Clarke
Matilda Stokes. Perfect. I caught
her on the way up, guys. Just like
I did with you, Skye. I can see it
all – rising stars, both of you.
Skye's our little dreamboat,
Mattie's our dark horse.

Skye
Well . . . she's no horse.

Clarke
Skye, you're a goddess and
everybody white already knows that,
but you need widespread appeal.
Black charts are still charts and
Ms. Matilda here holds the key.

Baron
I'm taking a break.

Clarke
No no wait wait! We can squeeze out
two more, Baron, I'm sure we can.
I'm sure you can!

Baron
What's Soul Train over here going
to do?

Clarke
Well, we're just getting to that.

Baron *plays a few notes of 'Coal Black Mattie'.*

Baron (*singing*)
'Coal Black Mattieee.'

Clarke *unceremoniously smushes* **Baron**'s *piano keys.*

Clarke
Yes, very good.

Baron
Well, figure it out and call me back
in.

Matilda
I really am sorry for interrupting.
I know that must be just the most
awful thing to do –

Skye
It happens all the time.

Baron

Does it?

Clarke

Interrupting?

Skye

Yes, Clarke.

Baron

You didn't see that? During the song?

Clarke

I was . . .

Baron

Paying close attention like you always do.

Clarke

Planning, Baron, planning so this evening is worth all of our while. Don't you want your while vigorously worthed, Baron? Or do you have to be somewhere else?

Baron

You've been down here too long.

Clarke

Just an hour, same as you.

Matilda

An hour? Oh no, am I late?

Clarke

You're right on time. Wanted to get the real 'Americana' out of the way so we can move on down to funky town and hear what you brought.

Matilda

I'm not sure –

Skye

But we're taking 'South' again?

Clarke

Oh god no, we don't have the tape.
But it sounded immaculate, Skye,
honestly.

Baron

Sure, but the end – clank, stomp,
'I'm terribly sorry!' – it's a
little avant-garde even for you.

Clarke

Don't ever accuse me of avant-garde
again in your life.

Skye

What was that, Baron?

Baron

Pardon, princess?

Skye

Was that a snuck-in compliment of
my singing?

Baron

I didn't hear one.

Skye

You agreed with Clarke's
assessment.

Baron

That's like agreeing with a
rooster's assessment of a sunrise.
You start to wonder if there's much
critical thinking involved.

Skye

I thought you were taking a break?

Baron
  I am.

Clarke
  Nope! We can do more.

Skye
  So 'When Things Went South' again.

Clarke
  It was truly fine.

Skye
  I don't want fine. I want wall-to-
  wall, Clarke. Hit machine. That's
  what you're here for.

Clarke
  And you'll have wall-to-wall, Skye.
  This was an exquisite addition to
  that wall's . . . breadth. It was
  soulful, it was tuneful, it made me
  think about every ill that plagues
  good people on planet Earth, and
  it'll appeal like hell to a massive
  swathe of . . . Americana-philes.

Baron (*scoffs*)
  'Americana.'

He finds this an unusual term to apply to music.

Clarke (*defensive*)
  Yes.

Skye
  Well, there's more where that came
  from.

Baron
  First you're slaves then you write
  the book on the place.

Clarke
Sure thing.

Baron
Then in many ways, back to slaves
again. For the most part.

Skye
Heady.

Baron
While we redcoats make money over
here. Again. Good for you, Clarke.

Clarke
Next up –

Baron (*to* **Matilda**)
Matilda, my dear, I'm fascinated –
what do you think about 'Americana?'

Skye (*without looking up*)
All that matters is how she sings it.

Matilda
I think Clarke's right.

Baron
About what?

Matilda
Sorry, I mean . . . it's . . . people
find it very appealing. That . . . style.
All over. Here too. Blacks and
whites. I mean originally it was –

Clarke
They certainly do! Thank you! Who
couldn't? And we're taking that
appeal and we're running with it.
It's a hybrid! She's doing a hybrid
sort of a deal. Texicana.

Baron

That's not a real thing.

Clarke

You could say that about anything
before someone invented it. And
Skye and I, we are inventing the next
ten years of Old World/New World
cross-country country sound.
Matilda, when you hear 'Townsman
Ferry' you won't know what hit you.

Matilda

I'm familiar with Skye's music.

Clarke

Of course you are. Of course she is!
She's an aficionado. *Aficionado Negro*.
I studied Italian.

Skye

Clarke. Over here.

Clarke

Yes, yes. Matilda!

Matilda

Clarke?

Clarke

Join us, won't you? Let's fill these
rusty musty halls with talent and
tape recording.

Skye *takes* **Clarke** *aside and locks eyes with him. She does not lower
her voice.*

Skye

She's a real peach and everything,
Clarkie, but why has Black Beauty
joined us? She a friend of yours?

Clarke

A new one, Skye. She sings, she
crafts, she arranges! She'll rock
you from a down-home country
princess to a bona fide sunny-side
soul queen like we talked about.
Trust me, honey.

Neither **Skye** *nor* **Matilda** *seem enthused by this.*

Skye

'Soul queen.'

Clarke

Soul queen.

Skye

That was your term.

Baron

Okay, I am taking this break.

He gets up to go.

Clarke

Trust me.

Matilda

Soul queen?

Clarke

Ready?

Matilda

For –

Clarke

For your first song?! Skye, come see
what she's brought. Baron, sit down.

Baron (*petulant*)

No!

Clarke

Oh good. You're rebelling. I'm sure
your friends are all very proud.
Sit down.

Baron

Fuck off, Clarke.

Clarke

Words, Baron, words I cannot hear
in here. I've said my piece.

Baron

You certainly have. But, Clarke?

Clarke

Yes?

Baron

Fuck off.

Baron *leaves.*

Clarke

Baron, I – this will only take a
minute.

Clarke *goes after* **Baron** *and exits.*

Clarke (*going offstage*)
BARON!

Three

Skye and Matilda

Skye *sits in a different corner of the room. Closes her eyes, as if she's
a cat, sleeping upright.*

Matilda

Fun bunch?

Skye
You have no idea, sister.

Matilda
I . . . I thought you'd have more of a posse, if you don't mind my saying so.

Skye
Oh?

Matilda
Just – from what I read. Your Village Voice interview.

Skye
You read that?

Matilda
I read everything I can.

Skye
You like my kind of stuff?

Matilda
I liked 'Papa' and 'Blue White Red', of course. 'Townsman Ferry' is one of my favourite songs in the whole genre, I must have worn that single out on my turntable. And I saw what you were going for with 'Isle of Skye' last year, I liked it. I've been looking all over for a copy of –

Skye *has her eyes open now – which slightly startles* **Matilda**.

Skye
You're lying.

Matilda
N-no, I –

Skye *rises and begins gathering up her guitar.*

Matilda *gives her room.*

Skye *absent-mindedly scratches the upper area of her left arm through her jacket.*

Skye
Maybe I do have a posse, kid. Maybe they just didn't want to spend all night five floors down in a second rate studio down a back alley in picturesque Burton Ames.

Matilda
Understandable.

Skye
They'd be here in a snap of my fingers, I just need the focus tonight.

Matilda
I wouldn't call Everglade second rate. It's got history, it's one of the oldest –

Skye
I just need the focus tonight.

Matilda *reaches into her case and withdraws some sheet music.*

Matilda
You want to see these?

Skye
Would love to.

Skye *leafs through them.*

Matilda
I think you're in a really interesting place, I mean, with where you could take the whole –

Skye
Who wrote these?

Matilda
Oh, well, a few people, some
friends –

Skye
Who?

Matilda
And some are kind of, started out
as more traditional kinds of –

Skye
Was it you?

Skye *stares bluntly at her.*

Matilda
I – the writing, you mean?

Skye
If you wrote them, just say you
wrote them.

Matilda
I . . . some of them really are based
on traditional . . .
Yes, I wrote them.
With some help. On some of them.

Skye
Good. Good. That helps me decide . . .
if they're a good fit.

Skye *smiles, with no warmth at all. She continues inspecting the
sheets.*

Matilda
It's your session, I'm just, here
to . . . To –

Skye *looks up.*

Skye
> To . . . ?

Matilda *smiles nervously.* **Skye** *looks back at the sheets.* **Matilda**
thinks, then gathers up her confidence and is about to reply.

Matilda
> To –

Skye
> Let's do them.

Matilda
> Oh, great – which?

Skye
> All of them.

Matilda
> All? I thought this was just an A
> and B side thing?

As **Skye** *sets up the studio for a recording, she pushes* **Matilda***'s
songbook and other papers to the floor and sets up the music she
intends to play.* **Matilda** *picks them up.*

Skye
> It is, it is, but look at what
> everyone's doing these days.
> Endless singles, B-sides,
> additional material, secret stuff.
> Fans, and I'm going to have oodles
> of them the second this one hits,
> they're going to want to hear every
> bit of tape with my voice on it
> that's ever existed.
> That's where the money is going to
> be. Churning up obsession. You
> pause too long to wonder if you
> like where it's going and suddenly
> you're going nowhere.

She finds a sheet she likes and holds it up.

Matilda
I suppose that's right . . .

Skye
Clarke called it something I liked –
we hit this right, this next go
around, we're in golden slumbers.

Matilda
Oh, I just loved that track.

Skye
Which one?

Skye *is reading over one song.*

Matilda
The – /

Skye
/ I'm feeling lucky. Let's record
this!

Matilda
Oh, I like that one. It's one I –

Skye
See that big important-looking desk
over there?

Matilda
Yes!

Skye
Run over and hit the big red
button.

Matilda *does this and the studio starts to record.*

The red light illuminates again.

Skye *plucks her guitar to the melody, learning the song from sight.*

Matilda *distributes music sheets to the piano and other music stand.*

Skye *begins to sing into the room's central mic.*

Matilda *sets up the second mic, which* **Skye** *does not notice.*

Skye (*singing*)
Been sixteen hours on terra firma
Seen more of life than I ever had
before
I'm learning more, yearning for
That big blue sky I much adore
So don't be such a high-chin bore
Give this city girl a chance

Matilda (*singing*)
Show me that charming country cool

Together (*singing*)
Throw up your hands and dance

As **Matilda** *joins in,* **Skye** *is taken aback at her audacity but continues singing.*

Matilda (*singing*)
Show me you ain't nobody's fool

Together (*singing*)
Give this city girl a chance

Skye (*singing*)
Give this city girl a chance

Four

8:27pm

Clarke *and* **Baron** *enter, still quarrelling. Hearing the music, they stop arguing and* **Clarke** *shoves* **Baron** *towards his keyboard.*

Skye (*singing*)
Now I ain't learned to square dance
just yet

And don't you hold your breath
I will
But when the timing's right,
One sunlit night
We'll sway away in sundown's light
I'll give you one last kiss tonight
If you give this city girl a chance

Baron *finds a place to join in on piano.*

Together (*singing*)
    Show me that charming country cool
    Throw up your hands and dance
    Show me you ain't nobody's fool
    Give this city girl a chance

Matilda (*singing*)
    City girl, city girl

Skye (*singing*)
    Come on, boy, give me a whirl

Matilda (*singing*)
    City girl, oh, city girl

Skye (*singing*)
    I may come from a different world
    But give me one last moonlit twirl

Matilda (*singing*)
    City girl, city girl

Clarke *celebrates silently in the corner.* **Baron** *gestures to him to turn the pages.*

Skye (*singing*)
    The city's blocks and towers
    Can make me feel alive
    But to while away the hours,
    drowsing
    On a bed of dogwood flowers

Shows me there's more to life than
nine to five

Together (*singing*)
Show me that charming country cool
Throw up your hands and dance
Show me we ain't nobody's fool
Give this city girl a chance

Matilda (*singing*)
City girl, city girl

Skye (*singing*)
Come on, country boy, show me how to
twirl

Together (*singing*)
Show me that – country cool
Throw up your hands and dance
Show me you ain't nobody's fool
Give this city girl a chance

Matilda (*singing*)
City girl, city girl

Skye (*singing*)
Come on, boy, give me a whirl!

Matilda (*singing*)
City girl, city girl

Together (*singing*)
Give this city girl a chance.

Nice finish.

Matilda *beams.* **Skye** *can't help but smile.*

Clarke *bursts into applause.*

Clarke
Tell me we have all that!

Skye
We do.

Clarke
Angel!

Clarke *goes behind the desk and stops the recording.*

The red light's out.

Baron (*to* **Matilda**)
Not bad.

Skye (*staring away*)
Thanks, Baron.

Baron
Both of you.

Clarke (*to* **Matilda**)
Did you write that?

Skye
She had help.

Matilda
I, well I reworked an old . . . I made
it more 'Skye'.

Clarke
Damn right you did!

Skye
What's your next trick?

Clarke
I thought we wanted a break?

Skye (*locking eyes with* **Matilda**)
That was Baron and that was before.
Before Top of the Pops here woke us
up. I want to hear more from the
little genius.

Matilda

Oh, really it was just –

Clarke

It was brilliant, Matilda. Exactly why you're here. What is next?

Matilda

You're too kind –

Clarke

Hear us –

Matilda

It's really just a little –

Clarke

No, hear us. It had such flair, such soul, a vision that matches our vision. I loved it. It was free, it was yes, it was us, it was now, it was here, it was Skye – I loved it, what's next?

This doesn't land well with **Skye**.

Baron

'Soul and flair . . .'

Matilda

Well, I tried to bring in what I thought Skye would like –

Clarke

Great.

Matilda

And for her range and audience, and, well, audiences I see and hear around me. I mean people are so delighted to feel a sharing in their art, you know? A sense that we're making it together, that there's a conversation to music, a

welcome and a listening ear. It's
not just about making a statement,
it's about making a statement
together, and making that statement
together is in itself the statement
we want to make, and what they want
to hear!

Clarke
. . . Great. Well, we need something
pretty churchy, for the religious
nuts. Do you have anything like
that?

Matilda
Churchy?

Clarke
Yes.

Matilda
I think I do.

Clarke
Groovy! This bodes well. As things
bode, this bodes well.

Clarke *bounds back over to the booth.* **Matilda** *sorts through her
sheets and withdraws a good option.*

Matilda
Skye, I have a few that might,
well, it depends, we could . . . well
first I have to ask, are you –

Skye *silences her.*

Skye
Easy.

Skye *withdraws, scratching her upper left arm through her jacket
again.*

Clarke *notices and waves* **Matilda** *over to him.*

Clarke
What?

Matilda
Is she, is Skye . . . ?

Clarke
Don't take that personally. She's
an artist. Manners are optional.

He checks his watch.

Matilda
No, I mean, is she . . . religious?

Clarke *thinks.*

Clarke
No idea. Just start singing.

Matilda
What?

Clarke
Start singing!

Clarke *hits record.*

Red light on.

Matilda
But – do we want –

Clarke *snaps and points to the light.*

Matilda *looks around, picks up a tambourine, then hands it to*
Baron.

He looks at **Skye***, who's enjoying* **Matilda***'s lost expression.*

Matilda *claps a bahbah-bah beat out to* **Baron***, demonstrating the*
Gospel-tinged tone of the song. **Baron** *begins playing along on the*
tambourine. Though he plays on beat, he's visibly unconvinced.

Matilda *takes the sheet music and places it on* **Skye***'s stand. She*
smiles slightly at **Skye***, who slowly acquiesces and starts strumming*
along to the beat.

Skye *turns to* **Clarke**, *who is already scribbling away at his notepad. He gives her a cursory grin and thumbs-up, then returns to his notes and headphones.*

Skye *turns back around. Out of respect,* **Matilda** *hangs back from the mic, as* **Skye** *looks over the lyrics on the sheet and prepares to sing.*

Clarke, *satisfied and excited, leans back in his chair, closes his eyes and clasps his fingers behind his head, calmly ready to record another winner.*

Just as she's about to raise her voice, **Skye** *pauses, still strumming, and grins at* **Matilda***. She gestures to the mic and steps back.*

Matilda, *glancing at the red light as time runs out on the song's build up, steps forward at the last second to sing.*

They perform 'Gone Flying'.

Matilda (*singing*)
   On the banks of Galilee
   All the kindness given me
   By the Lord of harmony
   We'd gone flying, out to sea

When he hears **Matilda** *singing, not* **Skye***,* **Clarke**'s *eyes snap open. He spends the rest of the song irritated and trying to gesture for* **Skye** *to sing and* **Matilda** *to back off.*

Baron *is loving this.*

Matilda (*singing*)
   Oh, we'd gone flying
   We'd gone flying
   We'd gone flying
   We'd gone flying, out to sea
   Gadarena, she was called
   And her soul from heaven has
   fallen, oh, Lord
   We'd gone flying in Jesus' name

Together (*singing*)
   Cast her demons to the flame

She glances back at **Baron**, *who's impressed, really enjoying it. He encourages her on. With newfound confidence,* **Matilda** *sings with a little more strength.*

Matilda (*singing*)
   The river Jordan –

Baron *begins to sing along.*

Baron (*singing*)
   The river Jordan!

Matilda (*singing*)
   Flows to sea –

Skye (*singing*)
   Flows to sea . . .

Matilda (*singing*)
   Walk with Jesus, Peter 'n' me

Matilda *smiles. Noticing she's getting sidelined,* **Skye** *pushes into the first mic to sing:*

Skye (*singing*)
   We'd gone flying
   Spirits clean

Matilda *sings louder, despite* **Skye**.

Matilda (*singing*)
   Take her down to glory be

The song in full swing now, **Baron** *tosses* **Matilda** *the tambourine and dashes to the piano to accompany.*

Together (*singing*)
   We'd gone flying
   We'd gone flying
   We'd gone flying
   We'd gone flying, out to sea
   Sunset shining
   All the same
   Off Gadarena's heavenly mane

Skye (*singing*)
   Hell's a reaching

Matilda (*singing*)
   For your soul

Skye (*singing*)
   For your soul

Matilda (*singing*)
   Burn it out, Lord, oh take control!

Together (*singing*)
   Gadarena, sin no more!

Matilda *really shines, entering this Gospel-rock character with charm and ease.*

Together (*singing*)
   We'll go flying, out the door

Matilda (*singing*)
   Flesh and blood and journey whole

Together (*singing*)
   Return in glory, to your home

Skye (*singing*)
   To your home

Together (*singing*)
   Oh, we'll go flying
   We'll go flying
   We'll go flying
   Back on home!
   Back on home!

Matilda *and* **Baron** *coordinate a triumphant ending.*

Matilda (*singing*)
   Back! On! Home!

Baron *finishes the performance with a flourish,* **Matilda** *grins ear to ear. A lovely moment.* **Clarke** *bluntly stops the recording.*

Red light out.

Five

Good Work

Baron
Good work!

Skye
Soulful.

Clarke
What the heck was that?

Matilda
What?

Clarke *comes out from the booth.*

Clarke
Did you notice anything, Matilda,
about that recording that might not
exactly be the assignment tonight?

Matilda
I'm sorry, I –

Clarke
Skye was barely singing at all!

Baron
Oh come on.

Clarke
I barely heard a peep!

Baron
Leave her alone.

Clarke
You were singing more than her!

Matilda
I'm not sure –

Clarke

No, I can see that. What is the
point, kid, of arranging music for
a rising star, if that star does
not move an inch in the process?

Skye

I'm tired.

Clarke

I'm sure you are.

Matilda

I'm sorry.

Clarke

I'm sure you are too.

Skye

Clarke –

Clarke

And another thing, while we're on
the subject, I barely heard what we
have you in here for. Which is
what?

He stares her down.

Soul. Don't forget that.

Skye

Clarke –

Baron

That was soulful as fuck, Clarke.
Don't be a nob.

Skye

How many more?

Clarke

A couple more, then we break for a
bit, okay?

Skye

Clarke . . .

Baron

Clarke, she can barely stand.

Clarke

Deep breaths, kiddo, deep breaths.
Baron, get her some water.

Baron

She's really out of it, look.

Clarke

If you want her taken care of, get
her some nice cold water now.

Baron

You've got a fucking problem.

Clarke

Yeah, and I'm looking right at it
and it's not getting water.

Matilda

Is she alright?

Baron

Does she look alright?

Clarke

I've seen worse.

Baron

She's green!

Clarke

I've seen greener. I've seen
greener strike gold.

Clarke *and* **Skye** *lock eyes.*

Clarke

Gold, Skye . . .

Skye

One more.

Clarke

Yeah?

Skye

One single, one more.

Clarke

You got it. Room! Room, we're
vibrating, let's make it a good
vibrate and not a bad vibe, okay?
Okay?

Matilda

Okay.

Baron

The sooner we finish this . . .

Clarke

How about a quiet one. Wunderkind,
I'm sorry I yelled. What do you
have ready for us that won't break
Skye but still, you know, features
her?

Clarke *observes some of* **Matilda***'s music sheets.* **Matilda** *has
an idea and looks through her collection.*

Skye

What's going on here?

Clarke

What do you mean, sugar?

Matilda *finds the sheet she was after.*

Matilda

How about this?

Clarke *breaks away from* **Skye** *and pays full attention to* **Matilda***.*

Skye *goes off to her own corner, away from them.* **Baron** *observes her.*

Clarke
Is it good? What is it?

Matilda
It's good.

Clarke
Soul?

Matilda
Yes.

Clarke
Flair?

Matilda
I hope so.

Clarke
Good enough.

Clarke *brings the sheet to* **Skye**, *presenting it as a peace offering. She takes it and he touches her arm – an attempt at reassurance. Unclear how well that worked.* **Clarke** *returns to his desk.*

Skye *walks back to the mic.* **Matilda** *gingerly takes the sheet back and hands* **Skye** *the sheet with the guitar part. She smiles at her.* **Skye** *ignores her and reads over the song.*

Clarke *looks at his notes, then returns to the mics. He picks up the second mic and positions it a few inches farther away from the main one. He looks flatly at* **Matilda** *and gestures for her to stand by the second one.* **Matilda** *nods curtly and does so.*

Skye *watches this and smiles.*

Skye
Clarke?

While **Skye** *and* **Clarke** *are speaking,* **Matilda** *withdraws a very small flask and takes a subtle sip.* **Baron** *notices.*

Clarke
    Honey Pie.

Skye
    Can I change this?

She gestures to the sheet.

Clarke *reads it over, squinting.*

Clarke
    I don't know, I'm sure it's not a
    problem. Mattie?

Matilda *bristles almost imperceptibly at the nickname. Then she stands at attention.*

Matilda
    Clarke.

Clarke
    Can we change this? The words?

Skye
    Your words?

She smiles a fake, sickly smile.

Matilda *nods stiffly.*

Matilda
    If, if it, feels right.

Skye
    To you? Or to me?

She stares.

    Because you know, if you let me
    change the song, even one word,
    then I wrote it, too. That's okay
    by you? Half and half? That doesn't
    bother you.

Matilda

I'm happy to share.

Clarke

Gonna be half of nothing if we take
much more time on this.

Baron

What do you mean?

Clarke

Let's get in gear, that's what it
means.

Skye

Chin up, now. Got to have thick
skin down here, girl.

Matilda

I've noticed.

Clarke

Some soul this time!

Clarke *returns to his desk and hits the red button.*

They perform 'On the Train Station Platform' – **Skye** *sings lead,*
Matilda *sings backup.* **Baron** *joins in, observing* **Skye***'s slipping
the whole way through.*

Skye (*singing*)

She came back, from pickin' cotton
I came down on the noontime train
She went back to the house
you were caught in
We shacked up
and we was raising Cain

I went back,
caught a flight to the city
My brother's just wrapped up
some business in town
I told him about her,

he said 'don't you worry'
But when I told my mama,
she could not hide her frown

Time heals all wounds,
love weathers all storms
But I could tell
on the train station platform
She had your eye, she had your eye,
You gave me a kiss
but the end of us was born

I didn't sleep,
couldn't take time to think
There were too many options
and all of them felt bleak
It's a waking nightmare
when your boy's eye's a wandering
And you ain't nearby him
to settle that score

Time heals all wounds,
love weathers all storms
But I could tell
on the train station platform
She had your eye, she had your eye,
You gave me a kiss
but the end of us was born

Baron *plays the instrumental break.*

Skye (*singing*)
    If I'd been 'round that boy,
    I'd settle that score, oh,
    how I'd settle that score . . .

Skye *starts to waver. Her voice falters and she seems to be having trouble with her breath. She tries to sing the next line, and almost does, but she can't get there.*

Everyone notices. **Clarke** *and* **Baron** *are unsure what to do.* **Baron** *keeps playing.*

Matilda *takes over.*

Matilda (*singing*)
Way back when, way back when
I could tell
on that train station platform
She had your eye, she had your eye,
You gave me a kiss
but the end of us was born

Time heals all wounds,
love weathers all storms
I think I knew
on that train station platform
She had your eye, she had your eye
And we ain't had it no more

Skye *stares at the light until it goes out. She places her guitar down.*

Skye
I am going on a very overdue break.

Clarke
What?

Skye
Make do with the dark horse 'til I
get back.

She storms towards the door.

Clarke
Now hold on –

She whirls around.

Skye
What do you think you're doing?!

Clarke *darts his eyes to* **Matilda** *then back to* **Skye**.

Clarke
Me, or . . .

Skye
You, Clarke. Come here.

She storms out of the studio.

Baron *stands.*

Baron
Is she leaving?

He looks around for the time but sees there are no clocks in the room.

Clarke
No.

Baron
It's late, Clarke! I don't know how
late but I know it's late!

Clarke
Sit down, Baron.

Baron
Tell her that!

Clarke
Baron, shut up.

Clarke *scribbles a few notes as he gets ready to follow* **Skye** *outside.*

Baron *berates* **Clarke** *meanwhile.*

Baron
You really, you suit each other!
Both of you. Dreamboat and the
little brown besuited barnacle
clinging onto her.

Clarke
Baron, shut up.

Baron (*to* **Matilda**)
    He's so cute, isn't he, when he
    thinks I'm being mean.

Clarke
    No, you're being rude. Keep being
    rude and I'll acquaint you with
    mean.

Baron
    Oohoohoo.

Clarke
    You know what I like about you? You
    have so many opportunities to be
    interesting, Baron, and so often,
    you're just, not. See you in a bit.

Clarke *goes after her, but* **Matilda** *catches him on his way.*

Matilda
    Clarke, can I –

Clarke
    What?

He composes himself.

Matilda
    Did you like –

Clarke
    Yes, it was great. More of that.

Matilda
    I had some other ideas, I could set
    those up?

Clarke
    What kind of stuff?

Skye (*from the other room*)
    Clarke!

Clarke

Yes, just set up whatever.

He turns to go, then stops. He turns back around and walks up close to **Matilda**.

Clarke

But don't, um . . . we don't need
anything too . . . you know . . . you get
me . . . we don't need any real hard
Black music. Or, African, or
whatever. I should have said.
Nothing, street. That's the only
'eh' area. It's not really her . . .
you know.

Matilda

Right.

Clarke

Soul, but not, yeah, you get it. Sam
Cooke, not, the scary ones. We want
the whole . . . pops with the kids,
turn it up in the car, but we also
want moms to buy it, so . . . Grand.

Clarke *walks out.*

Matilda *and* **Baron** *watch him go.*

Six

Matilda and Baron

Baron

You've never worked with Clarke
before, have you?

Matilda

No.

Baron
Piece of work.

Matilda
He's . . . enthusiastic.

Baron
Like a cartoon cat.

Matilda *smiles with a little laughter.*

Baron
People like you don't usually talk like that, do they?

Matilda*'s smile is a little tighter this time.*

Baron *tries a warmer approach.*

Baron
I mean he's, you're . . . we can all see you're doing, you're doing this well.

Matilda
Th-thank you, Baron.

Baron
You are welcome, Matilda. Mattie?

Matilda
Matilda.

Baron *nods.*

Baron
Right.

Some moments of silence.

Matilda (*singing*)
. . . 'Coal Black Mattie . . .'

Baron *smiles eagerly and sits up. He thinks, then plays some lines of 'The Man Selena Loved'.*

Baron (*singing to himself*)
  Matilda was the sister, I knew I –

Matilda
  I'm grateful. To Clarke.

Baron
  Really.

Matilda
  This is my first studio session.

Baron
  How are you liking it?

Matilda
  I think I have to like it.

Baron
  Well, teach me. Miracle we haven't
  both choked on Miss America: UK
  Edition yet.

Matilda
  You don't like her?

Baron
  To put it mildly.

Baron *walks around the studio, checking the wiring and audio
equipment, because he knows no one else will.*

Matilda
  I was thinking I'd ask her to help.

Baron
  Ha!

Matilda
  What?

Baron
  To help . . .

Matilda
With having Clarke see what I'm
trying to do here, I feel like I'm
being breezed over, is that unfair?

Baron
Oh, no.

Matilda *looks around the room for a chair or a stool. She was never offered one to begin with.*

Baron
It's not a bad tactic, though.

Matilda
What do you mean?

Baron *mimes taking a sip of alcohol.*

Matilda *blinks.*

Matilda
I don't . . .

She sees that he knows.

Seems to work for everyone else.

Baron
I won't tell.

Matilda
I'm not having any more. It didn't
sit right. I never usually –

Baron
We've all needed some cowboy
confidence, especially at . . . What
time *is* it?

Matilda
I think if she listened, if Skye
just listened, it could really move
both of us forward.

Baron
　Best of luck securing that
　partnership.

Matilda
　Why?

Baron
　Check her left shoulder next time
　you get the chance.

Matilda
　Her shoulder?

Baron
　You're better off appealing to
　Clarke, mad as that may sound. At
　least he likes your . . . soul and
　flair.

Matilda
　Soul . . . I never.

Baron
　Never what?

Matilda
　I've never heard it said so many
　times by one person and mean less
　and less each time.

Matilda *opens her bag for a handkerchief and withdraws her small flask.*

Baron
　Welcome to proceedings down here.

Matilda *offers the flask to* **Baron**.

He thinks, then grins and takes it. He puts it down on the piano as they talk. He never gets the chance to actually swig any.

Matilda

Clarke seemed really . . . open, when
we met, and still does, but –

Baron

Listen. You know that saying? That
piece of wisdom, it's a small point
about a small thing, but aren't
they the most revealing? It's when
you're sitting with someone and
there's a jug of water. And you
each have a glass. And this wisdom
goes, it's a really telling thing
how you pour that water into that
glass. What order, I mean. If we're
sitting together and I pour that
water into my own glass first, then
yours, some would say I'm an anti-
social member of society. Then
again, if I poured your glass
first and then mine, I'm an
upstanding citizen.

Matilda

I hadn't heard that but I believe
it.

Baron

Now, Clarke. Clarke will pour your
water first and look you square in
the eye while doing it.

Clarke and **Skye** *start to come back.*

Matilda

Okay –

Baron

But then he'll fill his glass up
higher.

Baron *takes a coat off a stool in the back of the room and hands it to* **Matilda**. *She silently thanks him.*

Seven

Is She Okay?

Clarke *and* **Skye** *return.* **Clarke** *seems to be slightly propping* **Skye** *up from behind.*

Baron *hides the flask in his pocket.*

Clarke
    Okay! Upwards and onwards.

Skye *is visibly breathing deeply.*

Baron
    Is she okay?

Matilda
    Skye, are you alright?

Skye *turns as if to leave but* **Clarke** *gingerly intercepts her.*

He stares into her eyes.

Clarke
    Yes.

Skye
    . . . Yes.

Baron
    Clarke, your pretty little cash cow
    is heaving out her million-dollar
    lungs and you're counting pennies
    on the rental.

Clarke
    You think we're in penny territory
    here?

Baron

Judging by the furnishings, yes I
do.

Matilda

The point is she needs some kind of
attention I think.

Baron

Exactly.

Clarke

You don't even like her.

Baron

I've managed to go eight years
without watching someone die during
a session and you of all people
should know that's fucking hard to
do. I'm not breaking that streak
now.

Clarke

Mister Dramatic.

Skye

I can do another. It's just the
air.

Clarke

The air.

Matilda *finds the music for 'The Air That I Breathe.'*

Baron

Let her go upstairs!

Matilda

She said she could do another.

Clarke

True.

Matilda
Can you do another?

Skye
I can. Give me a moment.

Matilda
We don't have that much time, right
Clarke?

Baron
You think you're gonna get any good
material out of her in this state?

Clarke
Yes, Baron, I do.

Baron
She's fried! Or at least, fry-ing.

Matilda
She'll be fine.

Baron
Clarke, you don't know what she's
going to do next!

Clarke
No one knows what anyone's gonna do
next. That's how you know you're in
the present. That's how you know
you're alive.

Baron
Well, at this rate she's not gonna
make it through the night. Then
where will you be?

Clarke *considers.*

Clarke
One more.

Baron
Christ.

Clarke
Then a big nice break.

Matilda
How fast do we need to go?

Clarke
It's not all time, Matilda, it's
tape. We're promised to deliver a
set of recorded content of at least
arguably outstanding quality, and
that's all I can tell you right
now, so –

Skye *has been staring at* **Matilda**.

Skye (*to* **Matilda**)
Take that off.

Matilda
Sorry?

Skye
That.

She points to an item of clothing on **Matilda**'s *person.*

Matilda
My –

Skye
Yes. I don't like it. I'm not
playing until you take it off.

Baron
Clarke?

Matilda *and* **Baron** *both look to* **Clarke**.

He stares and thinks.

Clarke

... Matilda, make this easy, please –
could you?

All eyes on **Matilda**. *She slowly removes it.*

Satisfied, **Skye** *lowers her arm.*

Skye

Let's see if you know 'Townsman
Ferry.'

Clarke

I think we've recorded that one
more than enough times, sugar.
Matilda, let's try another one of
your –

Skye

She said she knows my music. Let's
see if it's true. Get some of that
old black magic on my biggest tune.
That ought to sell it, right
Clarkie?

Clarke

... Right.

Skye

Get my name out there in Harlem
Square.

Clarke

Matilda, are you familiar with the
song Skye is referring to?

Matilda

Of course.

Clarke

Baron, you know it?

Baron
I fucking arranged it for her.

Clarke
Then let's hope you know it.

Skye
Know what you're on, kid?

Matilda
I'll keep up.

Clarke
She'll keep up! Attagirl.

Skye *closes her eyes and prepares at the mic.*

Baron *subtly offers* **Matilda** *the flask. She shakes her head 'no'. He hides it again.*

Clarke *waits for everyone to be in position and starts recording.*

Red light on.

They perform 'September Waltz' (a.k.a. 'She Caught the Townsman Ferry').

Skye *locks eyes with* **Matilda** *and sings.* **Matilda** *tentatively adds backup.*

Skye (*singing*)
Up on the hillside
I watched evening descend
As my love in her down-coat
Disappeared 'round the bend
She packed up in a hurry
She said I'm not to worry
But up on that hillside
I watched it all end

Skye *motions for* **Matilda** *to sing along.*

Together (*singing*)
She caught the Townsman Ferry
I thought that I saw her wave back

But the fog in the sky
Must have misted my eye
And that shake in her voice
Hailed that unholy choice
That choice made for her
That September the fourth

Skye *motions for* **Matilda** *to stop singing. She continues to stare at* **Matilda***, then wanders from her mic over to* **Matilda***'s, with an eerily zombified gait.*

Skye (*singing*)
We dug and we planted
We held and we hurled
We tried every trial
Known to this world
She smiled, she had courage
Defiled and discouraged
That old rusty ferry
Was her last ticket out

Skye *runs her white finger across a part of* **Matilda***'s skin. The disrespect is palpable.*

Skye (*singing*)
And so she caught the Townsman
Ferry
I thought that I saw her wave back
But the fog in the sky
Must have misted my eye
And that shake in her voice
Hailed that unholy choice
That choice made for her
That September the fourth

Skye *seems to be drifting farther and farther from reality as she continues through the song.*

Skye (*singing*)
Down on the streetside
I search for the culprit

Who tore down my love
Off her angelic pulpit
It didn't take long
To get into some wrong
And shake out that demon
From the depths of this town

She lurches towards **Matilda** *and sings into her mic like a lunatic.*

Skye (*singing*)
He cried and he hollered!
He clawed and he braced me!
As we sank into squalor
I felt God as hell chased me
But I heard the ferry's ringing
And her bells they were a singing
As the dark turquoise bay took him
With a salty embrace

Baron *looks to* **Clarke**. **Clarke** *can't decide what to do.*

Skye *wanders back to the centre of the studio, but seems oblivious that she's way off-mic.*

Skye (*singing*)
Now when I watch the Townsman Ferry
I think I see him again
The fog in my heart
Walks me home after dark
And the shake in my voice
Hails that unholy choice
The choice that I made
That October the fourth

Skye *starts to falter.* **Clarke** *moves to help.*

Skye (*singing*)
I watch the Townsman Ferry
As the sea draws its veil
But it don't make no difference
I'm still watching it sail

Clarke *tries to gesture for her to get back in proper position but she's pretty far gone.*

Skye'*s eyes go wild, she stares upwards towards something invisible and massive.*

There is a change somewhere behind her eyes.

She begins singing the finale of an entirely different song – 'I Ride An Old Paint' by Charley Willis.

Skye (*singing*)
    Goodbye old paint,
    I'm leavin' Cheyenne
    Goodbye old paint,
    I'm leavin' Cheyenne

Everyone notices something's wrong. **Skye**'*s eyes are wild. Her voice is ghostly.*

Skye (*singing*)
    Ride around old paint . . .

Matilda
    Clarke?

Skye (*singing*)
    I'm leavin' . . . Cheyenne . . .

Skye *collapses.* **Clarke** *hits the desk. The red light goes out.*

Eight

9:01pm

Matilda *and* **Baron** *hurry over.*

Clarke
    Fuck!

Clarke *runs over too.*

Baron
    Take this girl to a hospital, now.

Clarke
Goddammit Baron, have you not been listening, we can't.

Baron
The hell do you mean by that?

Clarke
We can't.

Matilda
She'll be okay.

Baron
Stand up and look at me, Clarke.

Clarke *checks on* **Skye** *then stands away.*

Matilda
Skye look at me.

Baron
Clarke.

Matilda
She won't need the hospital.

Baron
I want to know what he meant.

Skye
Contracts.

Baron
What?

Everyone looks to **Clarke***.*

Clarke
That.

Baron
Excuse me?

Clarke

Your contracts. Mine too. This
session has to be finished, in a
timely manner. And we can't . . .

Baron

What?

Clarke

We can't leave here without
forfeiting, alright?! Every tape
here, every track I'm obligated to
have her and you record tonight has
to be done and dusted this session,
or we start to move into arrears my
company cannot pay for and
subsequently miss out on a payday
none of us can afford to skip out
on, alright? So, just, leave her be
and play your little instruments,
alright, Baron? Is that alright?

Baron

Have a nice night.

Clarke

Baron.

Baron

I'm not staying down here like some
trapped rat!

Clarke

Your money's hinged on it. You know
that, right? All of it.

Baron

Fuck off, Clarke!

Clarke

Every song you've prepared for
today, all expenses, last season's

outstanding numbers, it's all tied up in this. We record tonight, we all get something back and then some; if we don't –

Skye

We will.

Baron

Did you know about this?

Skye

My head kills.

Baron

Did she know?

Skye

Of course I know. I didn't think you'd be quite so whiny about it, but I thought it'd be best kept between me and management, nonetheless.

Baron

Your management, not mine.

Clarke

You're right about that.

Baron

What if she keels over again?!

Skye

I won't.

Baron

What's even the matter with you anyway?

Skye

Nothing.

Baron
'The air.'

Skye
It's nothing.

Baron
What did that mean?

Clarke
Nothing.

Baron *sniffs the air.*

Baron
You smell that?

Clarke
What's next?

Baron*s sniffs under his arm.*

Baron
It's something . . .

Skye (*to* **Clarke**)
My head still kills.

Clarke
Matilda, what's next?

Baron (*sniffing*)
Something . . .

Matilda *has set up to sing.*

Matilda (*singing*)
Some . . . tiiimes . . .

Everyone looks at her.

Matilda *sings the first line of The Hollies' 'The Air That I Breathe'.*

A beat. They don't find it funny.

Skye

Cute.

Baron

I don't know how well I feel now.

Skye *scratches her upper left arm through her jacket, more aggressively than before.*

Skye

Enough of the cute shit. Cute shit
is what's making me woozy.

Clarke

Right, yes! Good attitude. No more
shit. Especially not if it's cute.

Skye

We're doing a nasty one. Southern
fried from the rebel side. Real
music. My music. And I do not care
what the NAACP makes of that.

Baron

The what?

Skye

Selena. The love, the Selena, the
man. The song that we did. About
the sister.

Baron

Skye, you're spiralling. Clarke,
she's spiralling.

Clarke (*wavering*)

Spirals can go upwards.

Skye

Cue it.

Clarke

You heard her, cue it!

Skye (*to* **Matilda**)
Here.

She grabs the pages and thrusts them at **Matilda**.

Baron
Jug band setup, madam?

Skye
Just play good, Baron.

Matilda
Any particular –

Skye
Good.

Clarke
Skye –

Skye
We're staying down here til it's
all done, Clarke. So let's get it
done.

Nine

Let's Get It Done

She snaps to **Clarke** *to begin recording.* **Clarke** *hits the button.*

Red light on.

Skye *starts playing 'The Man Selena Loved'.*

Skye (*singing*)
Selena was the sister
I knew I never had
She had the kind of Devil smile
could turn an Angel bad
Could turn the yellow blossom
fields to a dark brown barren keep
Could hide a love of bein' loved
in a dead man buried deep

Baron *coaches* **Matilda** *when to come in and support with backing vocals.*

She's skeptical but sings along with him.

Skye (*singing*)
   So imagine my surprise
   I'd never seen Selena mean
   such sweet words before
   Her eyes burned like friendly fire,
   her lips sang like a dove
   But ain't no way to know
   what became
   Of the man Selena loved

Going full roots-rock maniac, **Skye** *gets more animated than ever.*

Baron *and* **Matilda** *sing 'bam, bam, bah-dum' underneath* **Skye**'s *heavily Southern-inflected performance.*

Skye (*singing*)
   Selena didn't surface
   nigh on thirteen days and nights
   She'd met the first boy
   she could trust,
   they set each other's hearts alight
   She promised he was good,
   she said she'd treat him fair
   She'd never shown me anything
   like that tender love and care

   So imagine my surprise
   I'd never seen Selena mean
   such hateful talk before
   Her eyes burned like feral fire,
   her lips cursed God above
   I knew right then and there
   what became
   Of the man Selena loved

We shovelled through the night
With our bloody hands
rough and sore
The southern moon sent silver rays
and I had never loved her more
At sunrise Selena looked at me
As I patted down the dirt
Her golden smile, her blazing eyes
Wiped away years o' hurt

Strumming her guitar with propulsive abandon now, she hits a climax with her playing and pulls off her guitar.

Baron *and* **Matilda** *continue the 'bam, bam, bah-dum' accompaniment and* **Baron** *continues thumping out the intense beat on the cajon. Both are perplexed where* **Skye***'s going with this.*

Skye*'s eyes are going wild; she seems a little possessed. She moves towards* **Baron** *and stamps her boots, indicating to go faster and hit harder.*

She then turns and advances on **Matilda***.*

Skye
 Stamp your feet!

Matilda *holds fast, just singing along.*

Skye
 I SAID STAMP YOUR FEET, GIRL!

Matilda *lightly stamps along.*

Clarke *wipes his brow with a handkerchief and does not see the following.*

Skye *grins and moves back to the centre . . . then takes off her jacket.*

A massive, freshly-applied, brightly coloured tattoo of the Confederate flag covers her upper left shoulder.

First, **Matilda** *does not notice. Then she very much notices.*

Matilda *stops singing along. She looks to* **Baron**, *horrified.* **Baron** *keeps playing, then notices and stops.*

There is an awkward halt in the song.

Clarke, *beginning to feel truly dazed, groggily looks towards* **Baron** *and gestures for him to keep playing.* **Baron** *does.* **Clarke** *still does not notice* **Skye**, *but notices* **Matilda** *and stares daggers at her for not singing.*

Skye *grabs her guitar back up and resumes the song with a euphoric snarl:*

Skye (*singing*)
 So imagine my surprise!
 When she walked 'way,
 right as rain,
 as she was before
 Her eyes burned like fateful fire,
 she knew when push comes to shove
 No one will ever know
 what became
 Of the man Selena loved
 No one will know what became
 Of the man Selena loved
 I'll make sure no one knows
 what became
 Of the man Selena loved.

She stands over **Baron** *as they bring the song to a blistering conclusion and finish.*

Clarke *stops recording.*

Red light out.

Ten

9:15pm

Skye
 Love that one.

Clarke
Matilda!

Baron (*to* **Matilda**)
I did say.

Clarke
That was a great take! Gold
standard, 'til you
whiffed it! What happened?

Matilda
What is that?

Clarke
What?

Skye
Oh, right.

Clarke *sees* **Skye**'s *taken her jacket off.*

Clarke
. . . Skye, I thought we said –

Skye
You said.

Baron
Cover it up.

Skye
Walk out like you've been
threatening all night if you don't
like it.

Baron
I don't like it.

Skye
I didn't ask.

Baron
Cover it up, Skye.

Skye

Careful how you talk to me.

Clarke *moves closer to* **Matilda**.

Clarke

Matilda, if you . . .

He trails off.

Matilda

What? If I what? Mind?

Clarke

Sure.

Matilda

You don't?

Skye

Look, I like your music.

Clarke

If you'd like to . . . go –

Skye

Some of it's great.

Matilda

Go?

Skye

I think I have one here somewhere.

Skye *ruffles through a stack of papers she left on* **Clarke**'s *desk.*

Clarke

If you'd like to?

Matilda

You just got through explaining
that if any of us go, we don't get
paid.

Clarke
  Right.

Skye
  Here it is.

Matilda
  And this record doesn't come out.

Clarke
  That's right.

Skye
  I wanna hear it.

Matilda
  I put a lot into this.

Skye
  Wanna hear it, Baron?

Matilda (*pointing at* **Skye**'s *shoulder*)
  I'm not going. But that does not
  make me happy to stay.

Skye
  I think it's Mary Wells.

Skye *squints one eye at* **Matilda**.

Clarke (*to* **Matilda**)
  That's great to hear.

Matilda
  Okay.

Skye
  Doesn't she look like Mary Wells?

Baron
  You tell 'em, kid.

Skye *finds 'Ain't No Gettin' (There From Here)'.*

Skye
> Maybe – Clarke! Maybe I should be
> singing these cute lil' songs like
> they were meant for. De-troit City.

Clarke
> Skye, let's get back to –

Skye *sings in an affected Black/'blues' voice. She's playing around, but no one else can laugh along.*

Skye
> De-troit city! . . .

Skye *thrusts the paper towards* **Matilda**.

Skye (*singing*)
> Tell me one thing, before you go . . .

Skye *looks* **Clarke** *in the eye.*

Skye
> Sound right?

She grins.

Skye (*singing*)
> Might be a hard question,

Skye *drops all playfulness and stares at* **Matilda**. *She holds out the lyric sheet.*

Skye (*singing*)
> Just give me a yes or a no . . .

They stare at each other.

Skye (*singing*)
> We been saying . . .

Baron
> Skye . . .

Skye (*singing*)
> We been saying . . .

Matilda *looks away.*

Skye
Fucking sing it.

Matilda *is frozen.*

Skye
I'm talking to you.

Matilda (*singing*)
F . . . forever . . .

Baron (*protesting*)
Clarke?

Skye
Good point, Baron. Hold that
thought, honey. Clarke? Material
should be recorded.

Clarke *hesitates, then runs to record.*

Red light on.

Skye
We need that, soul, of yours here,
love. Your line is –

Matilda
I know what it is.

Skye
Sing my part. Don't you want to?

Matilda *takes the sheet.*

Matilda (*singing*)
We been saying 'forever'
Going on a year
But the rate that we're going . . .
Ain't no gettin' there –

Skye
Real down-home, now. Like you're on
the farm. Like you're singing for
your supper, now.

Matilda's *voice trembles.*

Matilda (*singing*)
  Ain't no gettin' there from here

Skye *snatches the paper away.*

Skye (*singing*)
  Boys and girls have always promised

Matilda (*singing*)
  Girls say 'yes' when they mean 'no'

Skye (*singing*)
  Boys hear 'yes' when they want it, so
  be honest:

Together (*singing*)
  If you wanted that yes – then off
  we'd go

Skye *laughs and claps.*

Skye (*singing*)
  We been saying 'forever'
  Going on a year
  But the rate that we're going
  Ain't no gettin' there from here

Skye *waits for* **Matilda**.

Matilda (*singing*)
  Ain't no gettin' there from here

They finish. **Matilda** *is morose.* **Skye** *is nuts.*

Skye
  Now that was good. Ain't so bad
  being Black, babay. Might go take
  me a nap, excuse me, sugar-pies.

She starts to walk out.

Baron
  I thought she can't leave?

Matilda
  Yes, if she leaves don't we –

Skye
  I'm just down the hall, jackass!
  I'm not even leaving the floor.
  Hey! Cue up 'Blue Sky' – I feel
  like I need to teach you all about
  roots. The good stuff.

She grins and leaves.

Then she pokes her head back in. Nuts.

Skye
  And! And! It has 'Sky' in the
  title! Like me! HA!

She leaves again.

Eleven

Baron, Clarke and Matilda

Baron *stares daggers.*

Baron
  Other than that, Mrs. Lincoln, how
  was the play?

Clarke (*with a mirthless chuckle*)
  Huh.

Baron
  She doesn't seem right, Clarke.

Clarke
  She's tearing through 'em, I say we
  keep going.

Baron
  You'll keep going no matter what
  happens, won't you?

Clarke
We'll have to see what happens,
then.

Baron
Skye could come back here with her
hair in a Swastika pattern, you
wouldn't blink an eye.

Clarke
How would that work?

Baron
She could come back calling Matilda
here a n . . . a very bad word, and
nothing, eh?

Clarke *folds up* **Skye**'s *jacket neatly.*

Clarke
A very bad word.

Baron
Yes!

Clarke
Such as?

Baron
You . . . know!

Clarke *checks his watch.*

Clarke
Didn't she say cue up 'Blue Sky?'

Baron
Slave-driver!

Clarke
Baron!

Matilda *starts to laugh.*

Clarke *and* **Baron** *turn to her, confused.*

Matilda
    In this context?!

Baron *is mortified.* **Clarke** *cracks a smile.*

Baron
    Oh, oh I didn't even realize –

But **Matilda** *breaks into a full-body, infectious laugh.*

Baron *joins in.*

It starts to get a little weird.

Clarke *starts feeling odd about it.*

Baron's *laugh becomes a wheeze, then a cough. He has to sit down.*
Matilda *keeps on laughing.*

Baron *sits on the floor, wheezing.*

Baron (*softly*)
    I can't –

Clarke
    What?

Baron (*barely a whisper*)
    I can't breathe –

Clarke
    Baron?

Matilda *stares at* **Clarke**.

Matilda
    You knew she was . . .

Clarke
    What?

Baron *goes silent.*

Matilda
    Like that?

Clarke
You get used to it.

Matilda
I think I already am.

Clarke
No. You're not. I can tell.

Matilda *stares at him, then gets her flask back from* **Baron**'s *pocket.*

Baron *groggily wavers back and forth on the ground.*

Clarke *looks to the door.*

Clarke
Where *is* she?

Matilda *offers the flask to* **Clarke**.

He stares at it.

Clarke
I had a friend once tell me booze
only makes you fatter, dumber and
poorer.

Matilda
Doesn't sound like much of a
friend.

He looks up at her.

They watch each other.

She withdraws the offer of the flask.

Clarke
You're staying?

Matilda
My parents had a saying, they both
learned thirty years back during
clean-up. Around here, actually.

He watches her.

Clarke
   Yeah?

Matilda
   Can't explode the same bomb twice.
   And back then, they really meant
   it.

She watches him.

Matilda
   I'm staying. I want golden
   slumbers, too.

Clarke (*after a moment*)
   What?

Baron, *about to pass out, suddenly jerks his body and sits up, awake.*

Baron
   Where is she?

Matilda
   Miss America?

Baron
   Right.

Matilda
   Stars and bars . . .

Clarke
   Out.

Baron
   Right . . .

Clarke
   Just, wait.

Baron
   Oh I'm very fucking used to that by
   now, Clarkie!

Clarke
Well, good.

Baron *absent-mindedly fingers a small pocketknife, which the others don't see.*

Baron
Wait for her, wait for you, wait
for whichever second-rate small
town Stereo Sweetheart you bring
down here next to try and learn how
to sing.

Clarke
You know that's not true –

Matilda (*to herself*)
I wouldn't call her second-rate . . .

Baron
And even when –

Clarke
You know that's not true, *this
time*, if you'll let me finish.

Baron *slips the knife out of sight.*

Baron
No, she's the one! You were right.
Sky's the limit. This one's got
something that works.
And all you have to do to make her
really successful is . . .

He gestures to **Matilda** *matter-of-factly.*

Matilda *sings the refrain from 'The Air That I Breathe'.*

Baron
You think you're icebreakers, you
and Skye. You both expect the whole
world and everyone in it to part

for you like pigeons in Trafalgar
Square. And it's foul!

He blinks sleepily.

Baron
. . . No pun intended.

Matilda *starts laughing again.* **Baron** *joins in.* **Clarke** *chuckles a little.*

Clarke
Fowl.

Matilda (*to* **Clarke**)
What happened to 'Blue Sky'?! I
love that song.

She snaps at **Clarke**.

Matilda
Put it on.

Clarke (*unamused*)
Oh, good, yes I do too . . .

Clarke *walks over to the turntable and puts the vinyl on.*

Matilda *offers* **Baron** *the flask. He accepts.*

Twelve

Put It On

Matilda *fixes her eyes on* **Clarke**. *She moves towards him and pokes his chest.*

Matilda
You're gonna need to demand it,
Clarke.

Allman Brothers Band's 'Blue Sky' begins.

Clarke
What's that?

Matilda
Of us. Of Everglade. Of yourself.
While Princess is away. Are we
getting this done? Yes or no?

Clarke
Yes.

Baron
Probably.

Matilda
Yes.

A moment. The song reaches 0:17 at this line.

As if in a trance, **Matilda** *reaches out and strokes* **Clarke***'s face. Then she lightly slaps him.*

She grins. Her eyes are miles away.

Unimpressed, **Clarke** *stiffly laughs it off.*

Matilda *goes to slap him again. He catches her arm this time.*

Clarke
Okay.

Matilda *dreamily turns and notices* **Baron***, who gestures that she come away from* **Clarke***. She takes it as an invitation to dance, which she accepts, taking his hand. She twirls around him, then they move around together.*

Skye *returns, amused by the sight.*

Just after the second verse ends, around 0:46, **Skye** *speaks:*

Skye
Now she's got it!

Baron
She's had it all night!

Matilda *puts her arm around* **Baron**. *Led by* **Matilda**, *together they sing along to the chorus of 'Blue Sky'.*

While the song's instrumental break plays, **Matilda** *and* **Baron** *dance again.* **Skye** *invites* **Clarke** *to dance with her and they slow dance together in another part of the room.*

(This all takes place within the instrumental break from 1:08 to 4:13.)

Matilda *notices a key on* **Clarke***'s desk and leaves* **Baron** *to go take a closer look at it.* **Clarke** *spins* **Skye** *into* **Baron***'s path – they relent and dance with each other. Meanwhile,* **Matilda** *picks up the key and stares at the door of the studio. Transfixed by the lights behind the door, she slowly moves towards them in the background.*

The lights behind the door seem to glow and morph with bright colours. She turns to check if anyone else sees it, but they do not. She walks towards the lights.

Baron *collapses.* **Skye** *notices but keeps dancing.* **Clarke** *tries to help* **Baron**, *but* **Baron** *shakes* **Clarke** *off.*

Skye *takes the opportunity with them distracted by each other to flick through* **Matilda***'s private notebooks.*

Meanwhile, an offended **Clarke** *grabs* **Baron***'s shoulder.* **Baron** *turns and pulls out the small knife.*

Matilda *locks the door from the inside and holds the key tight in her palm.*

Clarke, *incensed, returns to the booth and withdraws a gun from a drawer. He walks over to* **Baron** *and sticks the revolver in his face.* **Baron** *meekly holds up the tiny blade in response.*

Skye *laughs and looks to* **Matilda**. *She notices her by the door.* **Skye** *stares.*

Clarke *starts to laugh.* **Baron** *starts to laugh, too. As they all double over in glee,* **Clarke** *keeps the gun in* **Baron***'s face and* **Baron** *keeps the knife up.*

Matilda *watches this, stone-faced, key in hand. She makes a decision.*

Suddenly **Baron** *and* **Clarke** *return to dead-serious confrontation, but* **Matilda** *walks between them, gently moving* **Baron** *aside by pushing him in the face.*

Matilda

We're finishing this tonight.

Clarke

Sure we –

Matilda

I am not asking I'm telling. I will
not have shared the same air as
Dixieland over here, all night,
without some guarantee it's taking
me somewhere. Right? Right Clarke?!

Clarke

Right! Well said. Groovy.

Matilda

It's taking me somewhere.

She holds up the key.

Clarke

Now I don't feel too good.

Baron

Kid.

Skye

'Dixieland.'

Clarke

Skye . . .

Skye *brazenly sings the beginning of 'Dixieland'.*

Skye
I WISH I WERE IN THE LAND OF
COTTON . . .

Matilda *puts the key on her tongue.*

Baron *and* **Clarke** *suddenly realise what she's about to do.*

Clarke
Mattie! Mattie, that's the only key.

She takes the key out.

Matilda
Matilda.

She puts the key back in and swallows it.

Baron *and* **Clarke** *lunge at her but it's too late.*

She gulps. **Skye** *bursts out laughing.*

Blackout. The music stops.

Thirteen

'Terror Underground – Part II'

The Documentary resumes.

Documentary (*voiceover*)
Crocidolite Monodium Grade 33-Dash
G-Three-Eight. Miracle fireproofing
binding agent, cuts thousands out
of building costs and weeks off the
race to meet a deadline. The ideal
shortcut in the short term.
But long-term exposure to CM-33-G,
say, all night in an underground
space, with a locked door and not
much elbow room, is all but a
guarantee for unsettling and
destructive behaviour.

Everglade Studio was practically
made of the stuff. It lined the
place.

Another Voice:
And this was known?

Documentary (*voiceover*)
It was relatively well-known. Sure.
The effects weren't but the slight
madness of the place was. Those
bottom two underground floors
should have been done years
earlier. It's one of the things
that got the entire building
condemned so quickly.
Well, that, and what happened down
there of course. Just after
midnight.

Act Two

Fourteen

12:37am

We return to find the studio in a state of disorientation.

All the music stands, microphones and furniture have either been toppled over or rest in a bizarre position.

Baron *stares into the red light, which now pulsates and glows in various eerie patterns.*

Clarke *is on the floor, reading a songbook that's clearly upside-down.*

Skye *and* **Matilda** *face each other, eyes locked.*

Psychedelic lights oscillate around the studio. We're inside the madness ourselves now.

The low hum of 'One of These Days' by Ten Years Later crescendos.

Skye *looks around the space and paces over to* **Baron***. She withdraws the knife from* **Baron***'s back pocket and turns towards* **Matilda***.*

Matilda *moves away and takes the gun from* **Clarke***'s desk.*

Skye *groggily accepts defeat and puts the knife down on a table.*

Skye *moves towards* **Clarke** *and takes his nearly lifeless face in her hands, inspecting his delirium. Then she rearranges him like a chair and leans against him.*

Their words are slightly slurred and erratic.

Skye
How many left?

Clarke
I don't know.

Skye
How many left, Clarke?

Clarke
As many as you want.

Skye *gets up.*

Skye
Get up.

Clarke
Skye . . .

She kicks him a little.

Skye
You heard me.

Clarke *stands up.*

Skye *points to the gun in* **Matilda**'s *hand.*

Skye
Get that for me.

Clarke *goes to* **Matilda** *and holds out his hand.*

Matilda
What was it you said?

Skye
Get it, Clarke.

Matilda *holds up the gun.*

Matilda
We're not finished.

Clarke
Almost.

Clarke *grabs it from* **Matilda**'s *hand.*

Matilda
Careful!

Clarke
It's alright, it's not loaded.

He checks the chamber.

Clarke
   Oh god, it is.

Skye
   Give.

Clarke *wavers, unsure whether to put it in* **Skye***'s hand.*

Baron (*not looking at them*)
   Don't do it.

Skye *takes the gun out of* **Clarke***'s hands.*

Clarke *turns back to* **Matilda***, then back to* **Skye***.*

Skye *points the gun at* **Clarke***'s head.*

Clarke
   Skye . . .

Baron *slams the turntable closed. The music suddenly stops and many of the psychedelic colours disappear. We're back in the studio. Some blues and purples colour the walls.*

The red light is still on.

Baron
   Do it.

Skye
   I could.

Matilda
   But we're not finished.

Clarke
   Skye . . .

Skye
   Get lower.

Clarke *sinks to the ground.*

Matilda
We need Clarke to be finished.

Skye
You can record it.

Matilda
I don't want to . . . I want to be
recorded.

Clarke
Skye, you –

Baron *comes over and lightly pushes* **Clarke** *over to one side.*

Baron
No more of that. We need him.

Skye *turns the gun and pushes it into* **Baron**'s *forehead. Pulling the trigger seems an even more real option now.*

Skye
Do we need you?

They freeze like that for a moment.

Matilda *moves forward and grips* **Skye**'s *wrist, giving* **Baron** *the opportunity to pull the gun from* **Skye**'s *hands.* **Baron** *places the gun on the ground, as* **Matilda** *trips* **Skye** *backwards, sending them both to the floor.*

Matilda *gets behind* **Skye** *and holds her arms.* **Clarke** *begins to laugh.*

Clarke
She's flying!

Baron *groggily moves to help. He holds down* **Skye**'s *legs.*

Baron
I've got her.

Matilda *and* **Baron** *sleepily restrain* **Skye**.

Matilda
  What's left?

Clarke
  I don't *know*.

Matilda
  You must know, Clarke.

Clarke
  Look at the tapes.

Matilda *goes and flicks through the papers in the booth.*

Realising she's free, **Skye** *groggily starts to get up but* **Baron** *reshuffles and holds on to her arms.*

Skye
  Oh you're a strong one, Baron.

Clarke
  I'm sorry, I don't know what's
  next.

Skye
  Get off me.

Baron
  I can't.

Skye
  Can't?

Baron
  She hasn't told me.

Matilda
  Two are left.

Clarke
  Skye, what do you want to –

Matilda
  I will choose what's in them.

Skye
Dirty, dark-eyed, fucking –

Matilda
And this is one that is in them.

She opens the turntable, takes out Ten Years Later's 'A Space In Time', and puts on a 7-inch of Donovan's 'Season of the Witch'.

Matilda
Do you like it?

Baron
I like it.

Matilda
I wrote it.

Baron
You wrote it.

Clarke
We should record it.

Matilda
We should.

Clarke
Are you breathing?

Matilda
I am.

Clarke
Okay.

Matilda
Are you breathing?

Clarke*'s unsure for a second, seems to pass out. He snaps his eyes open again.*

Clarke
Yes.

Matilda
　Okay.

Matilda *looks to the door. The light outside the door glows red and orange. She pauses, getting used to it.*

Matilda
　Are you breathing?

The lights appear to respond.

Matilda
　Okay.

Fifteen

Proud?

The studio seems to be illuminating **Matilda**, *following her lead.* **Matilda** *looks over at the table with the knife on it. She reaches for the knife, and takes it in her hand.*

The song finishes its first chorus, at 1:18, as **Matilda** *speaks.*

Matilda
　What was it you said before?

Skye
　You're a strong one, Baron?

Matilda
　Take it off, Skye.

Skye
　Move on.

Matilda
　I don't like it and I'm not
　playing until you take it off.

Skye
　What?

Matilda
That.

She points to **Skye***'s tattoo.*

Skye
You funny fucker.

Matilda *slaps* **Skye***.*

Baron
Hey.

Matilda
Hey presto!

Clarke
Careful with her.

Skye
Clarke! Get them off of me.

Clarke
Get off of her. She's . . . valuable!

Matilda
I don't like it and I am not
playing, until you take it off . . .
until it's . . .

Matilda *tries to clear her head. She walks towards* **Skye***. Still restraining* **Skye***,* **Baron** *stares at* **Matilda***, unsure what's coming next.*

The song hits 2:06.

Matilda
Until it's . . .

Skye
Clarke . . .

Matilda *stands over* **Skye***, grabs her left arm and pulls it upwards.*

Matilda
  Clarke?

Clarke
  Yes?

Matilda
  Record this.

As the song hits 2:15, **Matilda** *drives the knife into* **Skye***'s left shoulder.*

The lights are streaked with red and deep purple.

Skye *screams bloody murder as* **Matilda** *cuts into her skin and diligently slices around the Confederate tattoo.*

Baron *recoils in horror as it happens.* **Matilda** *finally finishes up and peels a sizable patch of* **Skye***'s skin from her flesh.*

The song intensifies in volume from 2:15 to 2:53.

Matilda *holds up the blood-drenched dangling patch of skin with the Stars and Bars clearly illustrated on it above her head. It glistens with viscera under the pulsating red lights and drips down her hand.*

Skye*'s in a mortified silence now, as* **Matilda** *gazes at the skin and wanders away towards the keyboard.*

Clarke *cowers away in a corner.*

As the song's instrumental continues, **Baron** *crawls towards the turntable and slams it shut around 2:54.*

The music stops and the nightmarish red lights disappear. The recording red light is still on.

Matilda *slumps against the keyboard, resting on the floor.* **Clarke** *crawls to his desk and hides under it.* **Baron** *sits hunched, in a daze.*

Skye *rolls over. Her left arm is a bloody mess. She stares upwards, wide-eyed, on her back. She turns her head to the side, sees the gun on the floor, and slowly crawls over towards it.*

Skye *reaches the gun, props herself up on a stool near the second microphone and levels the gun at* **Matilda**. **Skye** *breathes heavily. Her finger's pressed against the trigger. She raises it towards* **Matilda**'s *forehead.*

Matilda *looks down the barrel and smiles. Then she laughs. Then she stops. She opens her left palm, smiles and raises the freshly cut patch of* **Skye**'s *skin.* **Matilda** *slaps the patch onto her own forehead.*

It sticks.

Blood runs down **Matilda**'s *face and onto her teeth as she grins.*

Clarke *wretches.* **Baron** *turns away.*

Sixteen

??. ??am

Matilda *and* **Skye** *stare at each other.*

Matilda (*singing*)
  Show me that charming country cool . . .
  Throw up your hands, and dance . . .

There's quite a long pause.

Skye (*singing*)
  Show me you ain't no-body's fool . . .

Matilda *smiles.*

Together (*singing*)
  Give this city girl, a . . .

Baron *laughs.* **Skye** *lowers the gun.*

The patch of skin flops off **Matilda**'s *face and lands on the floor.*

Matilda
  Hope you won't be missing it.

Skye
    To tell you the truth, I don't even
    really know what I'm missing.

Matilda
    Not much.

Matilda *looks around the room. Takes a deep breath.*

Matilda
    I've got one more.

Skye
    We'd love to hear it.

Matilda
    Good.

Matilda *begins to sing the first verse of 'The Air That I Breathe' to Skye. Slowly and dreamily.*

Clarke *rests on his side.*

Baron *stares at nothing.*

Matilda *continues to sing the first verse.*

Matilda *surveys the room. Her eyes land on* **Baron**.

She stares at him until he notices. He gets her silent message and begins to crawl over towards the piano.

Matilda *begins to sing the second verse. She stands. Slowly and surely. She sings the last part of the verse.*

She sees that **Baron** *is in position at the piano. He gives her an inebriated nod.*

Matilda *sings the chorus.*

Baron *plays the song's triumphant crescendo on the piano.* **Matilda** *starts to hiccup as he finishes. Right at the piano riff's conclusion, she covers her mouth.*

Matilda *spits up the door key.*

It clatters to the floor.

Everyone stops and stares at it.

Matilda
   . . . Sorry.

Blackout.

Red light out.

The Hollies' original recording of 'The Air That I Breathe' resumes (at 2:51).

The End.